Contents

Introduction

Blizzard's new game has taken the gaming world by storm with millions of players enjoying the fast paced action, stunning graphics and immersive sound. If you are still struggling a little to get started or looking for some further tips to become a higher tier player, then the following 185 tips are for you.

When you start out, you many feel a little over-whelmed. There's a huge amount to take in on the screen and there are a lot of potential characters to learn about. Each has their own strengths and weaknesses. In addition to that there's more information to pick up about various game play modes and all the different maps.

Don't worry – this book contains all the tips, tricks and strategies you need for beginners and more advanced players alike. The book has tips for all the characters and their counters along with strategies for different game styles, maps and enhancing the settings for better performance. It also has the Top 10 tips of things to do and the Top 10 list of things to avoid every time!

Let's read on and get started!

Chapter 1 – Beginner Tips #1 - 17

Overwatch has proved extremely popular ever since its release with millions and millions of players enjoying its frenetic pace and non-stop action. It looks fantastic and can be totally immersive with many of its sound effects also giving useful clues for the action.

This introductory chapter contains all the beginner tips you need to get started effectively and most importantly of all - to enjoy playing the game from the very first moment you start your first game. This chapter isn't going to make you an immediate master, but it will introduce all you need to know to get started and not be at a total loss within the first few seconds.

Let's read on to see what easy tips we can follow to get the most out of the game right from the very beginning.

1 – Keep it simple to start. If you're new to the game, it's easy to feel a little overwhelmed. There is so much going on it can be difficult to get to grips with all the action. You might feel a little lost or disheartened. The best way to get through that process is to pick the right character.

Your choice of character matters because some characters are easier to control and get to grips with than others. Don't just leap into the first one that catches your eye. The following tips describe some of the top characters you want to choose for each of the four Hero categories: Offense, Defence, Support and Tank as you begin your journey.

2 – Start with Soldier: 76 for the first Attack Hero. If you're coming from other first person shooters, you are going to feel right at home with Soldier:76. He's the type of run and shoot player you will be used to seeing all the time. He packs an assault rifle with a rocket launcher and has a good turn of pace. His ultimate ability is

going to get you a lot of hits as well as it locks on targets for you. There's a reason he's the first character in the tutorial. Soldier: 76 is a great way to get introduced to the game before you think about moving on to more varied characters.

3 – Try out defense with Bastion. Bastion should really be your first choice for Defense hero. He's not as well regarded now as during the initial release, but if you can get him in the right position he can deal some massive damage to the opposition. Playing Bastion is a great way to get to know the maps and the important choke-points where he can hammer the enemy. This gives you greater knowledge for when you play other characters later on.

4 – Use Lucio as your first Support Hero. A regular favorite of many players, Lucio is able to use his natural agility to help teammates in many different situations. You can help your fellow teammates by giving them health or increasing their speed so they can reach the fray faster. Useful in so many ways, Lucio is a natural pick to have in any team.

5 – Try Reinhardt for your first Tank option. An easy choice for a tank hero, Reinhardt has a powerful shield which can cover everyone on the team. He might be a little slow but he is critical in escorting teammates safely around. Reinhardt has a good amount of health and is even more powerful once you have mastered the Charge. Don't even think about not having a Reinhardt on an Escort map.

6 – Remember you are in a team. Overwatch is not a game that rewards individuals running around solo and trying to rack up enormous Kill/Death ratios. Overwatch is a team game and as such it's important you pick your character according to the needs of the team. Overwatch will make a suggested choice for each game about what should go into a team. Feel free to ignore the tip for the benefit of the team. Situations and opportunities will vary. Be prepared to adapt your play and character according to the different scenarios in the game.

7 – If it's not working, then change. Overwatch is a game that actively encourages players to change their characters, however all too often you see the same players choosing the same characters even though they're getting destroyed every time. Unsurprisingly, the same thing happens all over again.

Be flexible and prepared to adapt both your player and your tactics to the appropriate game. Being stubborn and insisting on the same character will get you and your team nowhere.

8 – Be the support. If no-one else on the team seems prepared to step and be the support player, then you need to be the one. Support players are critical to any team's success. It's a vital role that is often ignored by players who want to run around and shoot all the time. This might work in other first person shooters, but in Overwatch you need someone to heal the team members.

9 – Kill the support. If support is so valuable for your team, it makes sense it's equally valuable for the opposition. Make it your priority to kill an enemy Lucio for example, before he can help his teammates or buff them. This will make it easier for the whole team to complete the objective.

10 – Talk to each other. Overwatch rewards communication with teammates. Try to agree on a plan as a team and tell each other where you are going and what you're about to do. Talk about the objective and work together.

11 – Be constructive. It's no good hurling abuse at your teammates. It will get you nowhere and only annoy or upset everyone. Working together is beneficial for everyone. Playing the blame game at the end of a loss will get you nowhere fast. Figure out how to improve and what areas to look at for the next time. You can mute other players who seem to find this concept difficult.

12 – Listen. Overwatch has plenty of audio hints that you can use if you are listening carefully to the battle. The most obvious of these is when an Ultimate is about to be launched. You will get a second or two to react beforehand. Bear in mind the audio announcement is different depending on whether the Ultimate is from a friend or

the enemy. If you're hearing a foreign language, it will always be the enemy callout.

13 – Learning maps. A deep knowledge of where everything is on a map will prove invaluable. Much of this will come with repeated practice, but be observant. Take note of little details that will inform you of your position as you navigate around. Observe also where the enemy is fond of hiding or particular routes they take. Most people act from habit and it's easy to get some extra kills when the enemy are repeating the same mistakes each time. Always try to remember where the health packs are as well.

14 – Headshots. Headshots cause twice the damage of normal shots in Overwatch (Widowmaker is the exception to this rule as she can deal 2.5x damage). A red flare on your crosshair will tell you if you've had a successful headshot as well as a slightly different sound. Ana, Reinhardt, Winston, Zarya Syemetra, Phara and Junkrat cannot headshot.

15 – Play with the same people if you can. Building up relationships can be rewarding with the game. Knowing your teammates' strengths and weaknesses will allow the team to function better. If you can play with your friends and form a strong unit that works together, you will have more fun as well as a lot more success.

16 – Personalise your controlling device. You don't need to stick with the default keys. Configure them so they work for you. All the abilities can be remapped to whatever key or controller button you like.

17 – While you can't kill your own teammates, you can kill yourself. Watch you're sensible with some of the characters' most powerful moves.

Chapter 2 – Heroes Tips #18 - 61

Overwatch has many characters you can play. If you're playing the game correctly, you may find yourself playing 7 or 8 characters in one game just to combat what the opposition is doing and to complete the objective as fast as possible. Overwatch is all about being prepared to adapt your style of play to suit the current situation.

In order to do that, you will need some tips about the various players and their strengths. This chapter looks at every individual hero and provides the two most important tips you need to get playing straightaway and capitalising on the advantages each of them brings.

18 – McCree can be lethal with flashbangs. Follow them up with Fan the hammer for a great combo attack. You can use Fan the Hammer twice in a row if using Quick Draw as well.

19 – McCree's Dead Eye can get to a lot of enemies as long as they are in the line of sight. It's ineffective against shields though.

20 – Soldier: 76. His ultimate, Tactical Visor, will conveniently aim for you which is helpful. His helix rockets are powerful as well and he can also heal.

21 – Soldier: 76 can sprint. Use it with the Helix Rockets to allow you to jump up to various previously inaccessible locations on the map. He can be used effectively even for simple moves like charging the enemy as both the Rockets and Pulse Rifle can cause serious damage.

22 – Genji's Swift Strike cooldown is reset without delay if he manages a kill or gets an assist.

23 – Genji is highly agile and manoeuvrable. You can get to a lot of places quickly and easily and the deflect skill will be invaluable against all incoming projectiles.

24 – Pharah can fly the longest out of all the heroes. Use this to aim for enemies who aren't moving around a great deal. The rockets are not quick though so try and go for a group of enemies rather than individuals running around the map. Make sure you use the splash damage on groups to full effect.

25 – Pharah can be taken down while in the air. You can also wait until she lands to kill her. Don't get caught within range of her ult though. It's one of the most powerful in Overwatch.

26 – Reaper is awesome at administering some serious close range damage, but as you can imagine, the shotguns are fairly useless over long distances. Use Wraith Form to escape if you find yourself trapped from afar. Consider Reaper against Tanks for big damage or getting to snipers who might have thought they were safe.

27 – If you're Wraith Forming you are invulnerable and can still grab some health packs if needed. If you're fighting against him, keep an ear out for his laughter indicating the teleport.

27 – You need to be constantly active with Tracer. Although she doesn't have massive HP she can nip in and out of enemy lines easily before they even realise what's going on. Don't even think about taking on heavy targets though.

28 – The Rewind ability can be great fun. You can use it get health back or simply avoid enemy ultimates. It can be highly effective at saving yourself and also dealing damage when combined with a pulse bomb.

29 – If you're playing Hanzo make sure you use the Sonic Arrow. It's very effective in revealing enemies in hiding. It works on the same principle as Infra-Sight.

30 – Hanzo's ultimate ability is lethal (and fun to use). Note that it can pass through walls easily so be sure to position yourself so you

can capitalise. If an enemy is in a tight space in a chokepoint, it's perfect.

31 – If you've ever used Bastion before, you'll be aware he can deal the most damage out of all the characters. With great power comes a serious lack of pace though. Try to at least keep moving as much as possible in order to get into turret mode. Avoid being flanked – effective placement is critical if you're playing Bastion. Note that you suffer twice the damage if hit from behind.

32 – Bastion is better at defensive play than offensive. If your team is hammering forward, you are going to find it hard to keep up, let alone have a chance to get into turret mode.

33 – Widowmaker's strength is as a sniper so you need to be constantly on the move and looking out for the best vantage spots. Beware if you're about to take her on in close combat though as she does have an assault rifle mode. Use her Venom Mine to alert you of intruder's presence and then polish them off with the assault rifle mode.

34 – The grappling hook looks cool, but it is also very effective to jump just as you are about to arrive. You end up leaping even higher which can surprise the enemy and give you some great kills if you can nail a snipe in mid-air.

35 – Junkrat has a great Ultimate ability – the RIP-Tire. This can cause some serious damage so once you hear the announcement of the ultimate you need to find out where the tire is coming from and leave. If you shoot it however, it will explode. Once you kill Junkrat, make sure you get out quickly as he can leave some nasty surprises in the form of grenades when he dies.

36 – If playing Junkrat, be sure to master his Steel Trap ability. This is powerful because not only does it hold other players in the same spot, but it administers damage at the same time. If you're crafty, you can place a mine in the trap and explode the mine while a player is unable to flee.

37 – Mei is great fun to play and is very powerful. The classic Mei combo is to freeze the enemy with your frost beam and then kill them with an icicle to the head. She can also help out her teammates by freezing the opposition and allowing everyone else to pick up the easy kills. A Mei playing with a sniper can be very effective indeed.

38 – Mei can also heal herself by using an Ice Block. This can often help you out if you can't find a health pack or a teammate to heal you.

39 – Her Ice Wall can be very tactically effective. You can use it to isolate enemies which then allows your teammates to go ahead and gang up on the single enemy. Just be careful you don't lock out your own players and leave them isolated. That won't make you very popular at all. The Ice Wall can also be used to block off corridors or get your teammates up to unexpected tactical positions.

40 – Torbjorn is really a defensive player who can use his turrets as well as giving teammates armor packs. If playing Torbjorn, you must get the turret upgraded as soon as possible. It's too easy to destroy at the base level. Get Molten Core on it as fast as you can. This will also allow you to attack and reload a lot faster.

41 – Sensible placement of the turret is critical. It needs to have line of sight but at the same time not be so exposed that it will immediately be destroyed if it's not upgraded. Get it to level 2 at least by hitting it with your hammer which will give you an upgrade.

42 – Lucio can be very useful when your team is confronted by an enemy ult. Using Amp It Up, for example, will help your fellow team members evade Mei's Blizzard successfully. His Sound Barrier can also give great protection.

43 – Lucio is also great at helping out the whole team. When you use Amp It Up you can give the entire team a boost so it's critical to keep a close eye on how everyone is faring. Because you are so fast it's also possible to sprint back to where you last died and help

out any of your remaining teammates still there with a useful health boost.

44 – Symmetra can hide some very sneaky turrets in unexpected places. Be sure to think carefully where the most effective locations might be for an advancing enemy. Small rooms are therefore ideal or perhaps near a chokepoint. As you can teleport away, you can always trick the enemy into a particular location before the turrets do their thing as you disappear. Remember the teleporter is fairly weak so it needs to be well hidden if it's going to last any length of time.

45 – Symmetra is great at helping out her teammates with shields. This is another way of giving health to your friends and the cooldown is very short on it.

46 – If you want to be a healer, then Mercy is the character for you. She can both heal and boost damage of her teammates so it requires you to be aware of who to heal and who to give boosted damage to. There's no point in healing characters who can heal themselves when it would be more effective to increase the damage they can cause such as Roadhog. In the same way, there's no point in healing teammates who are already at full health or close to it. You can still attack in those situations which will probably be of greater assistance to the team overall.

47 – You can only heal one player at a time so a good knowledge of who is in trouble is essential. Spread the help around to preserve the team as a whole, rather than concentrating on just the one person. Be sure to use your Resurrect ability sensibly. Resurrecting fallen teammates in an impossible position, where they will just get slaughtered immediately, is a total waste of effort.

48 - Zenyetta is not going to last long in a fight so play tactically and avoid those situations entirely. You will lose. Having said that, his Harmony and Discord Orbs can be really effective and help the team out immensely. You do have to keep a clear line of sight when using the Orb of Harmony though so be sure to communicate effectively with your teammates when using it.

49 – In the same way, tell your team when you use the Orb of Discord. If they all pile in once it's been used, it will make life a lot easier. Don't forget you can throw the orbs around as well.

50 – Zarya needs to be used for mid-range situation as she has no effective comeback against long range enemies. Her shields can be very useful. Whenever they suffer damage, Zarya's weapons charge which makes them more powerful. If you find yourself up against a Zarya you need to avoid attacking her when the shields are on. They don't last very long so position yourself accordingly.

51 – Her ult, Graviton Surge, can be really useful when combined with powerful teammates. It acts to draw in the enemy and administer damage, but will then allow the other players who can deal damage to close groups of enemies to step in. Did I mention already how important it is to talk to your team and let them know your tactics?

52 – Winston is ideal if you want to get into the middle of the enemy and cause utter confusion and mayhem while your teammates can step in and back you up. While his ultimate, Primal Rage, may not deliver the greatest damage, it is highly effective in pushing the enemy around and dislodging them from high places. It can be great fun to see them fall to their doom as they are caught up in the melee. The extra health you get at the same time makes you quite tricky to kill, but bear in mind that you can't use either your weapon or shield when in Primal Rage mode.

53 – Keep using your shield as Winston. It will protect both you and the rest of the team as you advance.

54 – Roadhog's most powerful weapon is his Chain Hook. This will shoot out at great range, grab an enemy and pull them towards Roadhog. Go for the weaker players such as Healers and eliminate them from the opposition team. Grab them and then ensure you get a head shot for the kill. He is also great at pushing players to their death.

55 – Roadhog may not have any armor, but he is able to heal himself with Take a Breather. Nonetheless, he won't offer massive

protection to anyone else on the team. When used to scout ahead and grab enemies from the side, he can be very effective though.

56 – Reinhardt is very strong. Out of all the available tanks, he is able to take the greatest amount of damage. His shield can take 2000 damage and will eventually be destroyed. Don't forget of course that you will still be vulnerable from behind. Ensure fellow team members have this covered for you. Roadhog for example can try and get round the side and grab you with the hook. You are all about leading the team and soaking up the damage or protecting turrets but don't be afraid to get involved in the fighting as well. Your ult will throw everyone in the way to the ground.

57 – Reinhardt's charge is great, but be aware that characters need to be more or less in front of you otherwise you will run straight past them. Try and get as close as you can before charging to limit the chances of the enemy evading the charge.

58 – One of D.Va's most effective moves is the self-destruct. Try to use it when the enemy are closely bunched together for maximum effect. She is also able to get a new mech very soon after the previous one has exploded with the Call Mech ult. Remember that she also has unlimited ammo while in mech. While more vulnerable of course by herself, she can still deal damage as long as she keeps her distance.

59 – D.Va's boost is also effective at getting around the maps and to unexpected places. The boost can also be used to knock players off ledges.

60 – Sombra's talents lie in evading the enemy and rendering them useless. By using her Hack ability, she can effectively nullify the opposition, which enables her or your teammates to step in for the headshot kill. In addition, use her to hack turrets. Sombra's a great team player and can be highly effective when used for objectives.

61 – Sombra's Thermoptic Camo will make her invisible but this ends as soon as damage is taken. Make sure to use it at the appropriate time. If it's in the middle of a firefight, it won't be of much use. Her translocator can be used anywhere on the map.

Chapter 3 – Counters Tips #62 - 81

Now we know the strengths of all the various players and the tips to play them, we need to know the best ways that we can defeat every character in the game. All of them have their own strengths, but these can lead to weaknesses as well which you can exploit through the right choice.

Some struggle when attacked from a distance. Some will find it hard to resist aerial attacks while others are strong but slow. Confusing them with rapid movement and swift strikes will bring great rewards.

Remember a tip from earlier in the book: don't stick to one character the entire game. Be prepared to adapt your strategy as the situation demands. If the opposition is making great progress with a tank based attack, consider what your options are. Perhaps they are hanging back and hitting you with sniper fire – who are the best characters to take down a Widowmaker player?

This chapter reveals the best counter for each hero and how you can use them to exploit the basic weakness for each player. No character is invincible. Blizzard have taken great care to ensure that every attack can be countered if you know how. Some of the character's skills and powers are either buffed or nerfed over various updates, but the information below will be relevant no matter when you play because it relies on the essential make-up of the character.

Let's read on to see how we can counter every character and attack in Overwatch.

62 – Genji can be very effective but he will struggle against Winston and Mei. Winston has a huge amount of health so can keep on going despite Genji's attacks. The most effective counter is

Mei however. She can use Freeze to counter any potential damage inflicted and then freeze Genji herself before killing him with a headshot.

63 – If you want to take down McCree then Widowmaker is your ideal choice. You want to be able to take him down from distance as he is too powerful at close range. He is also quite slow so Widowmaker shouldn't have too many problems in landing a shot at distance.

64 – Use McCree's flashbangs against Reaper and hit him hard at close range. You can also stop Reaper's ult if you use the flashbang effectively. Pharah is another option against Reaper. His shotguns lose their effectiveness at range.

64 – Pharah is another who is vulnerable to Widowmaker. Yes, she can get high in the air but she doesn't move at a great speed and a reasonably skilful Widowmaker should be able to hit her. Solider: 76 is another viable option alternative against Pharah.

65 – Solider: 76 loves to administer damage at close range so characters who can sustain damage head on with impunity are a good bet. Give Reinhardt a go against him or try to flank him with Roadhog and his hook and you should meet with reasonable success against the Soldier.

66 – Tracer's aim is to get into the fray and sow confusion wherever possible with her sheer pace and agility. She is in and out of the action all the time and can prove a difficult target to pin down. Even when she makes a mistake she can use Recall to get out of the error. However, she will find it difficult when stunned so a flashbang from McCree can work wonders against her. If you're very quick with Roadhog, you can also grab her with the hook. Bastion is another one who can be effective just by spraying bullets all over the place in the hope of landing a lethal shot.

67 – Bastion might look one of the toughest characters to try and counter, however there are several possible options open to you. You can go with Genji as a first effort. By using his ability to reflect, you can send the bullets straight back at Bastion. As he

can't move in turret form, he will be destroyed very quick by his own ammo. In addition, characters that are really agile and mobile will be highly effective against Bastion. The idea is to get in behind him and wreak damage as fast as possible.

Players that are able to teleport are another obvious way to counter Bastion. Reaper for example, can get right behind Bastion and immobilise him quickly as can Tracer. You could also try and go long range against him. Pharah's rockets can cause great damage from distance. Just make sure you never go head to head against him or you will struggle.

68 – Hanzo is not hugely effective at close range and prefers to administer damage from a distance. Tracer can get in there very quickly and confuse the situation while Winston can get stuck in at close quarters.

69 – On the other hand, Mei is hard to beat up close so attack from a distance. Pharah fits the bill perfectly here and can cause a lot of problems with rockets delivered from up high. Widowmaker should be another character to consider against Mei as well.

70 – Junkrat is pitiful against anything in the air. His grenades are useless meaning Pharah has free rein to counter highly effectively. Winston can also prove another viable option for getting in close and hammering him with the cannon.

71 – Torbjorn is easy prey to snipers. He is immobile so relies on very careful positioning, but if exposed he becomes easy prey. Pharah and Widowmaker therefore become the obvious counters as they can attack from distance with little concern of being hit from the turrets. Reinhardt can also offer useful defense for others to get in close if needed. Tracer can teleport in quickly, but snipers are usually your best option against Torbjorn.

72 – It can be a struggle to get up close enough to Widowmaker to finish her off, especially when she is adept at moving, sniping and moving on. Using speed to get in close before unleashing your weapons is the strategy you need against her. Genji is a good option, especially as the reflected bullets might kill her. D.Va can

move swiftly into position before attacking as well and is another good choice to counter Widowmaker.

73 – Zenyetta can smash through D.Va's defense matrix with the Orb of Discord and should certainly be a viable option to combat the Mech. The best route though is to pick Mei who can freeze her, which enables the rest of your team to pile in and destroy the mech. McCree with the flashbangs is also an option to temporarily disorient her, giving the team a chance to attack at close quarters.

74 – Reinhardt looks to be a tricky one to counter at first as his shield looks to be all encompassing. It will eventually get destroyed if you hit it enough, but it's more effective to play smarter and try and get in behind him.

Tracer and Reaper are the obvious candidates here who can get in at the rear where he is much more vulnerable. Even if he just turns around at least he's now moving the wrong way and may have forgotten that his primary purpose is to protect his teammates. You can bring a great advantage to your team by distracting him. Remember: it's all about the objective in Overwatch.

75 – Roadhog has immense power at close range with his shotgun as well as a very useful self-heal ability. His health bar does make it easier to gain energy from him though and allow the enemy to get to the ult faster. Using Mei against Roadhog is useful. You can prevent suffering damage by freezing yourself and then attack him. Reaper with dual shotguns is another excellent choice. The target is so large that it makes inflicting quick and heavy damage almost inevitable.

76 – Winston does look intimidating, however switching to Reaper is almost always going to be your best bet against him. Getting in close and personal with the shotguns inflicts massive damage and you can always get out when in trouble by using Wraith Form. Bastion can be another good option to pick if Reaper is not working out for you.

77 – Zarya is another character who relies on inflicting damage at relatively close quarters. You can nullify the effectiveness of her

attacks however, by shooting from afar. Pharah is a good option as she can attack from high up where Zarya's energy grenade is relatively weak. Work on the timing against Zarya. Attacks on her shield only serve to make her stronger.

78 – Lucio is a great support character. He's a healer and very mobile – a true asset to any team. The best way to counter him is to immobilise him. Use Mei to freeze him and then attack. Alternatively, the favorite move of McCree's flashbang followed up by his fan and fire ability will normally see Lucio defeated.

79 – Mercy is a very difficult one to counter because she is in the background so much assisting her team rather than playing a highly active role. Widowmaker attacking from distance is your best option with her, although you could also try a Tracer to get in behind her to attack.

80 – Symmetra isn't particularly strong, but her teleporter can really help out the opposing team by ensuring they get a shortcut back into the action. In many ways, it's more important to find out where the teleporter is and then move on to killing her. She has no chance against the power of Roadhog or Pharah and will lose very quickly in any kind of confrontation with those two.

81 – Zenyetta is slow and difficult to move around at any kind of decent speed. This makes him rather vulnerable to different kinds of attack. The obvious move is to hit him from distance with a sniper, but if you can get very close to him with a Genji or Tracer, he has no chance of being agile enough to escape either of them.

If you want to make serious progress in Overwatch, then a good knowledge of the maps is essential. You need to know where to pick up key objects, where the enemy might position themselves, the various routes, the best strategy for each map, the list goes on and on.

Much of this will just come naturally over time, the more you play. You will notice the same things happening over and over and players who are following similar tactics for each map. This makes them relatively easy to play against if you have a comprehensive knowledge of where to be at the right time.

This chapter will show you the various tips you need to improve your knowledge of the maps and how best to play them. The maps are currently divided into four categories. We will start with maps that are played in Assault mode. These are maps with a simple premise. One team has an objective which they need to control within 5 minutes. The opposing team's job is stop them achieving the objective. Let's start with Hanamura. This has the usual 5 minutes along with another 5 minutes of gameplay if capture point A is gained.

82 - When attacking, go as a team. Stick together and don't all disappear off in separate directions. This is the quickest route to failure on his map.

83 – Remember that you are playing an objective. Your primary aim is to get there and hold it. Worrying about kills or taking your eye off the ball to increase your kill count isn't going to help the team. It's worth repeating once more: Overwatch is all about the team play!

84 – Once you start capturing the point, the speed at which it is captured is dependent on the number of people you have on the

point. Capture it and stay there as long as possible with the team to press the advantage.

85 - When attacking there are certain players who will do very well on this map. Lucio will give everyone a speed boost which will enable your team to get there first. Every little step counts here in the race to get first position.

86 – Reinhardt is another key player here. Use his Shield to make solid progress against the enemy and push forward. The shield is invaluable, but don't forget he packs a mean hammer punch as well which will see off a few of the enemy who dare to get in range.

87 – If you're playing the defence in this game, keep focused on the capture point. Make sure at least someone is on it. This seems to be an area that many people have trouble grasping as they run off to kill the opposition, but it will make defending a lot easier if you remember the task at hand.

88 – You need a Bastion. He is essential when fortifying the double-gate location, which is a pleasing chokepoint to set up. Get Bastion set up there and possibly Torbjorn as well. Consider using Widowmaker from a distance as an additional defensive resource to guard against players trying to attack from behind. She will be well protected in lots of locations.

89 – Use Reinhardt against groups and also consider Mei. The Ice Wall is highly effective at blocking out points and her Blizzard can cause some big damage. Junkrat will also give you lots of effective defensive opportunities.

Temple of Anubis has issues for both the attack and defense. Here are some tips to help you get the most success out of the map.

90 – Bastion again will prove useful. He is of particular value when it comes to the defense of Point A though he can't do it all by himself.

91 – Again, when attacking you need to move as a group. Get a Reinhardt in there or a D.Va to facilitate progress as you are going to need a shield of some sort. This is particularly important for

Point B. You will have zero chance to take it, let alone hold it, unless you all go in together.

92 – Don't go out in the open. Stick to the alleys where you can. This is a map that snipers can do well on. If you don't have any protection, you can expect to get mown down fairly rapidly.

93 – If you're attacking, Junkrat is a good option although his traps can also cause havoc when placed effectively near spawns. Pharah is another powerful ally on attack and Zarya will prove equally useful on either attack or defense. Lucio is a must for both attack and defense.

94 – If you are after Point A, then having access to the arches is essential. If you can get that, you should be able to hold Point A. Without it, you have very little chance.

Volskaya Industries is another Assault map. It has a truck in the middle which makes it ideal for Roadhog to attack an enemy as he goes around the corner.

95 – When defending, try and capitalize on the placement of this truck. Establishing yourself behind it or with a secondary defense a little way back will give you plenty of opportunity to hold your own.

96 – Getting through that initial chokepoint at the first objective is very difficult. However, if you emerge from the spawn point on the left hand side, there's a platform over the water, under the yellow building. Not every character is able to cover the gap but the following are: Widowmaker, Genji, Pharah, Reaper, Tracer, Junkrat, D.Va, Winston and Lucio. Obviously some characters can do this more easily than others (those who can fly for starters!) so if you're stuck just opt for a D.Va for example, until you can master the others. It's a great way of sneaking up on the opposition however and causing damage.

97 – If you have a sniping character, get up high for some very strategic positions that will put the opposition in real trouble.

Watch out for flanking characters making their way through the map.

98 – Mercy is a good option for attackers as she can fly to the back of the map. Other useful attackers include Pharah, Reinhardt and to a lesser extent for this map, Lucio.

Chapter 5 – Control Maps Tips #99 - 109

The second category of maps are Control maps. Each one involves trying to be the first to capture and maintain a control point. The match consists of three rounds. To capture the point, there must be members from only one team on it. Once you have captured it, you will need to defend the point in order to get to 100% and victory. Bear in mind there's a 30 second delay before you can start capturing nor do you have to actually stay on the point to keep it.

99 – The Ilios map has a Lighthouse part which is perfect for snipers to sit at and hit characters as they emerge out of cover. It's a good place for turrets as well. It's well protected but the railings can be destroyed as well. Junkrat is a good choice here with his powerful grenades.

100 – Junkrat is also effective with the Ruins. The pit inside the Ruins does pose problems for defending as it is terribly exposed. Pharah will also have a great time here wreaking havoc. You need to get out of there if possible and stick to the sides or the top to defend the point.

101 – The Well is perfect for knocking people straight in which is good fun. A Lucio is great at this and Pharah will also prove useful with knock back from Concussive Blast. You can't go wrong with a Roadhog here as well and simply dragging people to their doom or a Reinhardt Charge.

Pharah is also good with surviving a fall as she can use her jump jet and Tracer can use Recall to get out of a fall entirely. D.Va can boost out as well.

Lijiang Tower is another Control map. It has three sections: Night Market, Garden and Control Center.

102 – Lucio is a strong player here. He can get there first which can help establish supremacy, even if you can't capture until 30 seconds of the match have elapsed. He can also push the opposition off heights to a deadly fall. Junkrat can prove useful too at attacking groups on a point with his grenades and Pharah will allow you to get to high points easily and can clear points easily from up high.

103 – D.Va can cause big damage up close as well as clearing a point. Mercy's Resurrect will come in useful on this map and in fact on all control maps.

104 – Avoid Widowmaker – she can't do a great deal here as there are few clear sightlines on the map. The same applies to Bastion. Symmetra adds little value either.

105 – Watch out for the balcony that looks out at the Control Center. Getting a good sniper in there can be very useful, but don't hang around too long or you will be destroyed.

106 – Take the quick route to the Garden over the bridge. Yes, it's more dangerous but it's worth the risk to try and get there first by killing the opposition on your way.

Nepal is another Control map. The three sections are Sanctum, Shrine and Village.

107 – Mei is powerful here with her Ice Wall that is great to block any kind of entrance. Junkrat can be good as well to lay traps and snipers or turrets have a decent line of sight.

108 – There's a chokepoint in Objective B at the gate which you can control if you get there first. If not, try flanking around through the buildings which will get you higher. This will enable a good sniper to cause damage and is a strong placement for a turret.

109 – Sanctum is another one that is great if you are using a player with any kind of knock back skill. It's relatively easy to send defenders to their death – just make sure you stay well away yourself. The use of the Concussive Blast from Pharah or Lucio again with his Soundwave is recommended.

Escort maps require a team to push a payload through a map and its various checkpoints. As the defenders, your role is to prevent the payload reaching its destination. You will have a small amount of time at the beginning of each round to establish your defensive positions. Every time the attackers get to a checkpoint, more time is added.

The more attackers that are with the payload, the faster it moves. You will also get a small health boost of 10 health per second by being next to the payload. Once all the attackers have left the payload however, it will move backwards after 10 seconds have elapsed.

Escort Maps require the attackers to get a payload through to its destination at the other end of the map. It's the defenders' job to stop them. There are two checkpoints to get through for each map. For the payload to get moving, there needs to be an attacker within range.

There is also an Overtime element in Escort. If you have an attacker in range at the point the time expires, you will get extra Overtime. This will give you a chance to get to the intermediate checkpoint. There are three Escort maps: Dorado, Route 66 and Watchpoint: Gibraltar. Here are some tips for each of them.

110 – There's a maximum time of 10 minutes for Dorado. You get five minutes once the map starts and then another 3 minutes if the first checkpoint is made. A final 2 minutes is added for reaching the second checkpoint.

111 – You can head to the left of the payload straightaway and try to outflank the enemy. Get the payload moving but be careful as you move round the corner you don't get picked off from high by snipers. You want to clear out the road because that first courtyard is going to be difficult if the defense already controls it.

112 – Make sure you continue to flank and clean out the side passages that surround you. Widowmakers will do well on this map as there are lots of sniping positions all around and on various rooves. Torbjorn can cover some of the wider, open spaces.

113 – Using Mei's Ice Wall can be of value on Dorado to completely halt progress towards the first checkpoint. Keep checking for health packs as they are fairly close to the path you will be taking. Learn the locations – this will prove invaluable knowledge.

114 – There's a balcony right outside the Compound. You can use this to leap in or keep the topmost sections clear for teammates to get through. Maintaining control of the higher ground should see you able to get the payload through it its final destination.

Route 55 has an American theme to it and was the final escort map added to the beta version. This is another map with quite a few varying routes and little paths to it. There are lots of ramps that seem to go all over the place, but each of them will lead to strategic positions. Having some time just practising moving around and getting to know the map will pay dividends later.

115 – As soon as you spawn you're going to face the music from snipers at distance – get yourself to cover as soon as possible. Even once you make your way past here, keep checking for snipers. There's a gas station with a roof on it that's perfect for hammering the advancing attack team This is an obvious place to try and own if you are the defence.

116 – The first part of the map is great for pushing enemies to their death. Cue the entry of Lucio. He is a great player to have in this map – in fact, he is essential to have on your team. Anyone who can push back or uses knock back is going to be valuable. Get a Reinhardt in there as well for extra pushing power.

117 – Once you start to make your way through the town, it's clear there are lots of roofs which are a viable defense spot. Turrets will prove useful here for hindering progress – Torbjorn can come in very handy.

118 – The final stage is good again for Bastion or Torbjorn who can be set up on the moving platforms for the defense. Using Pharah to try and destroy the defense who have tried to settle in, is a good option. If you're sniping as Widowmaker, be sure to stay moving. If you are still too long, it's easy to locate your position and get to you faster.

Watchpoint: Gibraltar is the final escort map. There are five minutes once the match begins. Every time you get to a checkpoint, a further 2 minutes are added to the clock.

119 – The payload could barely be in a worse starting position. A good start is vital if you want to have any chance at all. Go left to try and get around the building that looks out on the payload. If it hasn't had a lot of traps and turrets laid down, you might be fortunate enough to get through.

120 – Turrets continue to be of use throughout this map. Place them at the top of the ramp and they are going to prove difficult to get past.

121 – When attacking, there is not so much of a need to stick together in one place. In fact, if you can branch off a little and flank the sides for the first couple of stages, you will meet with some success in clearing out locations and allowing the payload to make progress. A Tracer can also give you a lot of help by getting in behind the enemy.

122 – The final two stages are going to be difficult for the attackers. Try to wrest control of the upper areas to rid them of snipers looking to take you down. Flanking here is going to be more difficult. Get a Reinhardt on the team who can offer some protection as well as charge forward against the enemy if the opportunity presents itself.

123 - Get a Bastion on top of the payload and stick Reinhardt right in front for a formidable combination. You can also use Symmetra's teleport to get right near to the payload each time.

Chapter 7 – Hybrid Maps Tips #124 - 147

The final category of maps are the Hybrid maps. These maps are a combination of Assault followed by an Escort scenario. There are four maps that fall into this category: Numbani, Hollywood, King's Row and Eichenwalde.

Let's start with tips for Numbani.

124 – If you're playing as a defender, then balconies are your friend in Numbani. Get on one which is protected by a tree. This will give you some additional protection. On the left of the payload as it advances you will find another one that gives you a great outlook over the approach and the right hand side which will enable you to pick off some flankers.

125 – If you are defending, the right of the payload is where you are going to struggle unless you defend yourself adequately. Widowmaker is an awesome choice here. Not just because of her sniping ability, but her spider mines will allow you some protection from attackers looking to sneak up on you.

126 – There's a large statue you will find quickly. Get yourself up there with the Hook and shoot between its legs for a great vantage point as Widowmaker.

127 – If you're attacking, Lucio is a good choice as is Mei who can block off sections of the map with her Wall. Lucio can sprint around the place as well as speed up the whole team if you're stuck at a chokepoint.

128 – Keep targeting the support characters here and watch out for Mercy and her resurrection ability. Controlling the enemy support is key.

129 – Keep communicating. As the payload won't go any faster once you have 3 players on it, you can use the others to fan out and try to outflank the defence. Try to gain control over the higher

areas and your progress will be much easier. Try your utmost to get to the balconies and walkways. This map is dominated by the higher locations.

130 – This is another map that is going to reward a deep knowledge of all the various routes and particular locations. Giving it a good go in practice is recommended although of course you will pick it up the more you play.

Eichenwalde is another Hybrid map that is relatively new to Overwatch. You need to get the battering ram to the Castle. It has different routes to the various locations and it will be of great use to know the fastest one to the different places.

131 – Eichenwalde is a great place to hide as the defenders and try to bait the attack out of their positions. Once they are in the open, it's relatively easy to kill them from a high vantage point. Tread carefully as the attack and be patient. You will make better progress with a more cautious approach. If you rush out to the middle of the exposed map, you will have no chance.

132 – If you're defending, you know the enemy are going to save their ult attacks until they get to the chokepoints. It's important you conserve yours as well, otherwise you will quickly find yourself pushed out of position. Once the attackers get on a roll, they will prove hard to stop.

133 – Use the higher positions but don't get stuck there. There are many spots on the map where you can stop as defense and rain down attacks on the enemy. They will attempt to flank you however, so it's a dangerous tactic to reside too long in the one place.

134 - This is a reason why Genji with his climbing ability can be a big asset to the attacking team. Pharah and Winston are also adept at getting through the chokepoints as they are so mobile. The better players are at moving vertically, the more suited they are to this map. Use them to distract the defense, allowing the rest of the team to make progress. Avoid Tracer on this map – her lack of vertical movement makes her of limited value.

135 – Remember to talk to each other. If you see the enemy coming down a flank be sure to alert your teammates. Equally, it you spot a potential opening, let others know. There are many good spots to defend but you will find yourself doing even better if you help each other out by communicating effectively.

King's Row is another hybrid map. This one is set at night in the streets of London with cobblestone streets. It starts with 5 minutes with a possible maximum time of 10 minutes, assuming no overtime.

136 – Being able to get up high is a massive advantage in this map. You will find Pharah exceptionally useful flying around and flinging down damage to the floor. She's great at warding off players from the payload.

137 – Get a Reinhardt in there while advancing to the first checkpoint and moving the payload. The streets are so narrow that his massive shield will cover just about the entire width of the street. As usual, he's vulnerable to an attack from the rear however. Couple him with a well-protected Mercy for a great combination.

138 – Get flanking if attacking. Reaper can sneak up on defenses from the side and Tracer can get in behind them all to eliminate some of the defenders.

139 – If you're defending, then snipers will prove useful. There are lots of various ledges in the final part which will enable you to get good shots in on advancing parties. Widowmaker is the obvious choice.

140 – Symmetra comes into her own on this map. Her turrets can be highly effective when placed in the correct position such as the entrance to the hotel lobby and re-inforce a deadly chokepoint. In addition, the extra shields will prove valuable as will her teleport in getting her teammates back into the action.

141 – You must have Mei in your team for this map. The Ice Wall is great at preventing any form of access whatsoever to the payload and can also distance the opposing teammates from each other.

This makes them easy pickings for your team to come in and hammer them. Her Blizzard ult will also prove deadly if she can block off an escape route.

142 – If you're looking to prevent the advancing enemy from outflanking you, then Junkrat will prove a good choice. He can send his grenades around corners and his traps will be awkward to avoid. The enemy should rightfully be fearful of his RIP-Tire rolling into view from around a corner.

Hollywood is the fourth hybrid map of the game. The payload is HAL-Fred Glitchbot and starts off in Hollywood Boulevard moving onto Goldshire Studios.

143 – Reinhardt will provide ample defence to the front as you advance through the line and will enable you to pass through the chokepoint. Couple him with Zarya for protection moving forward as well as against attacks from the rear. D.Va might also be a good option for the initial push.

144 – Vertical abilities are well rewarded in this map. Genji is therefore a good choice along with Tracer and Reaper.

145 – You can just move straight ahead after the archway, but it might leave you more vulnerable to attacks. Consider taking the staircase to the balcony for the high ground where you will be better placed to take on the snipers. Once you clear the way, you can keep on moving through.

146 – Lucio is valuable for the defence because of his speed buff for the whole team. This will enable defenders to make the journey back to the action faster. Lucio is also a good option for the attacking team on Hollywood to take out turrets.

147 – Widowmaker is valuable from afar as there are many balconies from which to attack. A McCree can prove deadly as well as there will be plenty of close action in this map and he does significant damage in the right situation.

Chapter 8 – Performance Tweaking Tips #148 - 165

This chapter contains various tips you can use to enhance performance on a PC and various character settings you can alter for different characters. If you're on a PC, you are probably used to trying to make the game look as good as possible without having a huge effect on performance.

There are also different character and in-game adjustments you can make that will have a dramatic effect on your own performance in the game. Let's look at ways we can modify these to enhance our own play and enjoyment of the game.

148 – Turn on the kill feed. It's vital you have this on display. It will give you a huge amount of information about what is going on in the game, who is struggling, who needs help, which of the enemy players are doing well and what you might need to do to combat the more successful enemy next time.

It really should be on by default, but you can make it appear by getting into the settings and the options menu. Turning this on will give you a big advantage in terms of getting the relevant information fast and being able to use it effectively.

149 – Customise the mouse. If you're using a mouse to play, then you will want to play around with sensitivity until you find a good balance between speed and accuracy. It's a personal preference, but if it's too high you will find it very hard to control. Even the slightest movement will send the crosshair all over the place. You will probably want to opt for a fairly low sensitivity to begin with.

150 – Optimize the resolution. You will be looking to get as high a resolution as possible of course with 1920x1080 a good choice. What's more important however is the frame rate so if you need to drop the resolution to improve it then consider doing so. You can

go down to 1280x720 and also to 720p if needed. You need to do your utmost to get to 60 frames per second for a good Overwatch experience.

151 – See as much as you can. The wider your field of view, the more of the game you will be able to see. The biggest number you can get to in Overwatch is 103. Try it on this setting and see how the game runs. The more you can see, the better informed you will be.

152 – Dynamic reflections. If you're having problems getting an adequate framerate, then this is a good set of options to change. You can turn off the dynamic reflections entirely if you like which should see a good frame rate improvement. Try it on Medium first to see what improvement you get. Ideally you would like to keep it to improve the look of the game and the extra clues you can get, but the framerate is more important. Remove it entirely if it helps you up to 60fps.

153 – Look at the fog detail as well to improve framerate. Drop it down as far as you need to see an improvement.

154 – The same goes for the shadow detail. Change the settings until you reach an adequate compromise.

155 – Consider dropping the render scale down as well. You will find this in the options and it may provide a good performance boost.

156 – If you don't need it, don't use it. Take a look at the other video settings, turn them off and see if it makes a big difference to your enjoyment or the information you are getting.

157 – Run the game without a border. A border can potentially add input lag.

158 – Get headphones. If you have a good pair of headphones, then get yourself to the settings and turn on Dolby Atmos. The number and details of audio cues in the game was mentioned earlier and you will be even better placed to pick these up if you have Atmos on. It can give you a vast amount of information that

will enable you to pick up all kinds of things you may previously have been missing.

159 – Change up the reticle. Choose a color that really stands out for you. This will vary from person to person, but don't just stick with the default. There are lots of different colors to choose from and some might be more suitable to different maps than others.

160 – Enhance pointer precision. Just turn this off. It can affect your mouse acceleration which is annoying when you've taken the effort to make it just how you want it. This is one area where many people struggle so it's important to take every step you can to get it right.

161 – Auto climb. This is a setting that is available for characters that are available to scale walls (Genji, Hanzo, Junkrat with his RIP-Tire). This is a lot easier than using the jump key as all you have to is run at the wall and you're on.

162 – Turn on Allied Health Bars for Solider: 76 and Zarya. Don't forget that these two characters are able to help their teammates. Turning on the health bars will enable you to see the state of the team and act accordingly.

163 – Widowmaker's Zoom. Widowmaker has a scope for her sniper rifle which you can also adjust for additional sensitivity.

164 – Change the crosshair. As well as the color, you can have a dot or a circle or various other settings that are unique to each character. This again is personal preference, but continue to experiment until you find one that suits.

165 – Adjust your preferences. You can change your button assignments so the controls for each individual character are different. You might want to switch around primary and secondary fire or the way different abilities can be accessed. This is a highly personal preference and depends on how you play, but continue to mix it up until you find the perfect combination. The right layout and button configuration can be the key to success or failure in Overwatch.

Chapter 9 – The Top 10 Tips To Do #166 - 175

We've already looked at over 160 tips for playing the game so far. This chapter considers what might be the top 10 tips overall. This chapter pays particular focus to tips both for doing well in the game and even more importantly, enjoying yourself while you play. If you're doing great, but not having a good time, there doesn't seem to be much point to it.

So here we have, in no particular order, the top 10 Overwatch tips!

166 – React to the conditions. Primarily, this means paying particular attention to the make-up of your team and making the appropriate changes. If the team needs a healer for example, then you should be prepared to step up and take that role. If you keep getting destroyed playing Genji because the map isn't right for him, then switch. Other games might reward stubbornly playing on and on and getting there through attrition eventually. Overwatch isn't that game. Always think about the tactical situation you are in and continue to change many times in the one match.

167 – Don't go in without support. You will find it very difficult, if not impossible, to make any progress in the game without adequate support characters. You need to work with the dynamics of the game and not against them. The support characters are there for a reason. Think how powerful a Mercy can be on the opposition – not only can she heal, but she can also resurrect. Look after the healers in your team. They are invaluable towards reaching your objective.

168 – Communicate. Yes, I know. It's been mentioned. But this tip simply has to go in the top 10. Talk, talk and talk some more to each other. You need to let your teammates know what you are doing and when you are doing it. Work together as a team rather

than a bunch of individuals doing their own thing and you have much more success.

169 – Use your ultimates together. If you are working as a team, then this should be easy. It's great to use your ultimate ability and it will have an effect, but this is intensified if you can use them together or one straight after each other. Timing is crucial and there won't be many teams that can sustain two or three ultimates when used together.

170 – Go as a team. Did I mention Overwatch is a team game? Go in hard together as one unit. If you try to attack a point as individuals you might make the odd one, but overall you are going to come off second best to a half decent defense. Get in there with your teammates and you stand a much better chance of success. Don't just trickle in.

171 – Keep on the move and use cover. If you're stuck in one place, you're going to die quickly. Keep mobile and you stay alive. Don't get penned into one location or reveal a favorite spot to which you keep returning. The enemy will be on it and you'll be dead before you know it. Movement is crucial.

Using cover is equally important. Wide, open spaces are trouble. They give great lines of sight to snipers and turrets and almost invite you to get shot. Use the cover you will find in the map wherever possible as well as the shields that your teammates provide. The more you play, the more you will learn about the key locations in the map. This will enable you to go long distances without taking the risk of getting shot from distance. This is also true if you head up in the air. Watch for those snipers…

172 – The sound is a great feature in Overwatch. Even if you're not using headphones, it still adds a lot to the game. Not only does it enhance the game, but you will also get lots of important information from the sound cues. They will tell you when to press and also when to retreat. The opposition ultimates have their own sound cues. Learn them and you give yourself a chance to escape just before they are launched.

173 – Learn the maps. Of course, the more you play the game, the more you will learn as you go and in a way it's hard to beat the pressures of a real game. However, a little time spent on your own exploring or playing with just one or two friends can be helpful. You can set this up under Custom Game which will let you choose maps and difficulty level along with lots of other settings. This will give you a lot more time to play and explore different routes and hiding places and locations. This information will serve you well in a more competitive game.

174 – Keep shooting. There is no running out of ammo or time spent reloading in Overwatch so you can shoot all the time. Don't forget that your ultimate continues to charge whenever you cause any of damage so a stray bullet here or there that does unforeseen damage can be really helpful. Clearly, if you're attempting to be stealthy, you need to adapt this free-shooting strategy accordingly. Equally, it doesn't hold true for every character – you'll need to change it up for snipers for example. In general, it pays to shoot.

175 - Enjoy yourself. To me it's the most important tip of all. Overwatch is meant to be fun. Everything about it, from its colourful action and sounds to team play to the non-stop pace of it all is designed to be enjoyable. If you're feeling frustrated or annoyed by the game or other players, then just take a break. Come back later and play when you're calmer. Make enjoyment of the game your number one priority and everything else will fall into place over time.

Chapter 10 – The Top 10 Tips Not To Do #176 - 185

We've looked at the top 10 tips of things to do, now let's look at what we should avoid to enhance our play and enjoyment of the game. Here are the top 10 tips of Overwatch "don'ts"!

176 – Don't focus on things that won't help the team reach the objective. An obsession with a kill/death ratio isn't useful. Forget things that won't help the team reach the objective and win.

177 – It's fun to get Play of the Game, but again, don't make it a primary objective. If you get it at the expense of your team winning, it's unlikely anyone is going to be impressed. Plays of the Game will come the more you concentrate on actually winning the game.

178 – Don't hoard the ultimate. Of course you shouldn't just use it as soon as it's been earned, but you sometimes see players go the whole game waiting for the perfect opportunity which never comes. Use it quickly and then work on getting the next one.

179 – Don't forget balance. Having 3 Meis in a game for example is not balanced. If you stack up the same hero in one team, you are unlikely to have much success. It is possible, but very rare. Spread the abilities of the heroes as widely as you can.

180 – Don't get hung up on personal vendettas. It may be tempting to hone in on one player who always seems to be killing you, but resist the temptation to pursue and destroy one player. Once you start doing that, you make what should be a team contest into a personal battle and forget the route to victory. Don't get side-tracked by things that won't help you win.

181 – You can of course solo queue (play by yourself), but it helps to be with friends (or ideally lots of friends). It's harder to play by yourself and will be more fun anyway, the more buddies you can

get. It will also let you establish tactics and strategies which you can implement over time together. Try and avoid solo queue if you can.

182 – Don't get disheartened or even think you should win every time. It's simply not going to happen. If you get upset every time you lose, you're really not going to have a good time playing the game at all. Look at your overall success rate and be sure to take one or two learning experiences from each loss to improve for the next game.

183 – Communication has already been mentioned as a key component of the game but do not fall into the trap of letting off steam by having a go at other players. There is no point in shouting or hurling insults at any of the other players. It makes the entire game less enjoyable for everyone and does nothing to help you either. In addition, there's always the chance you will get reported and blocked.

If you are really annoyed, take a few minutes break and come back later. Turn everything off and get some fresh air and come back when refreshed and when you're in the right frame of mind. Avoid becoming that "toxic" player that everyone hates to play with.

184 – Don't leave games early. For two reasons: it's annoying for the other players and it will also incur an XP penalty. You won't be punished for the odd game that is beyond your control but always try and see the match out once Assemble Your Team has taken place.

185 – Don't "not enjoy yourself". So important, it had to be in both lists. Have a great time playing Overwatch. Learn from each game and apply it each time to the next. You will get better and better the more you learn and the more you practise. Keep playing and always ensure you're having a good time!

Chapter 11 – Extra Bonus Content

Knowledge is the key to success in Overwatch. Knowledge of characters' strengths and weaknesses, their counters, knowledge of the maps, knowledge of when are where to make the right moves. One of the fun ways you can continue to improve your own knowledge of the game is to test yourself and your friends.

I have put here a few examples of the questions you will find in my Overwatch Quizbook: 500 Questions and Answers. I hope you enjoy reading this as well and I'm sure it will give you plenty of help as you continue to play the game. How many of these can you get right first time? The answers follow all the questions.

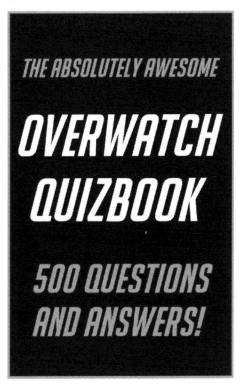

Attack Heroes Questions

1.   What is McCree's first name?

2.   What is McCree's job?

3.   What is his primary weapon called?

4.   What sword would Pirate enemies drop?

5.   What is the reload time for this weapon?

6.   What is McCree's ability which helps him reload while

     moving called?

7.   What is McCree's ultimate ability called?

8.   How much charge is needed for his ultimate ability?

9.   What does McCree use to stun players?

10. What does Fan the Hammer do?

Tank Heroes Questions

1. How much health does Winston have?

2. How much armor does he have?

3. How much damage does the Tesla Cannon do in a second?

4. How quickly can Winston move with his Jump Pack?

5. What does Barrier Projector do?

6. What is his ultimate ability called?

7. How long does it last?

8. How much extra health does it add?

9. What is the advantage of using Tesla Cannon?

10. When will Jump Pack stop straightaway?

Maps Questions

1. Who do you need to escort in the Hollywood map?

2. King's Row is a combination of two types of map. What are they?

3. What do you need to escort in this map?

4. In what country is King's Row?

5. What type of map is Oasis?

6. In what country is Oasis based?

7. What are the three sections in Oasis?

8. What do you need to do in Watchpoint: Gibraltar?

9. Where does the attacking side spawn in this map?

10. What are the three sections in Lijiang Tower?

Attack Heroes Answers

1. Jesse

2. Bounty Hunter

3. Peacekeeper

4. Cutlass

5. 1 ½ seconds

6. Combat Roll

7. Deadeye

8. 1500 points

9. Flashbang

10. Shoots any bullets in the cylinder widely

Tank Heroes Answers

1. 400

2. 100

3. 60

4. 20 meters a second

5. Protect Winston and anyone else while moving

6. Ultimate Ability

7. 10 seconds

8. 500

9. Automatic targeting of enemies

10. If you hit a wall

Maps Answers

1. HAL-Fred Glitchbot

2. Assault and Escort

3. An EMP device

4. England

5. Control

6. Iraq

7. City Center, Gardens and University

8. Get the drone to the rocket

9. Winston's Laboratory

10. Control Center, Garden and Night Market

Conclusion

I hope you have enjoyed this guide and collection of the best tips you will find for Overwatch. It's a great game that is enjoyable to play and rewards skill and practice. It's rare to find a game that is so rewarding for smart play as well.

To be successful in Overwatch, you need to be constantly aware and thinking about the situation. It's not a route to victory to run in and try to shoot everyone without a proper plan or some kind of sensible strategy. This is a game that rewards thinking. As such, it's not all about who has the quickest reflexes or the best set-up on their machine. Continue to think about what you are doing, working as a team and communicating together and you will quickly find a lot of well-deserved victories coming your way.

Above all, carry on enjoying the game. It's been great fun to play since the beta got released and to their credit Blizzard continue to modify and enhance the game with new releases all the time. It's continually evolving and reacting to the players so there's no chance of getting bored or feeling you have beaten all it has to offer.

I very much hope the previous 185 tips for Overwatch will prove helpful to you in your future gaming. I look forward to seeing you on the battlefield in the near future.

Best of luck!

James

59113097R00029

Made in the USA
San Bernardino, CA
02 December 2017